My Amazing Toddler
Behavioral Series

# I Am Strong.
# I Say NO!

An Affirmation-Themed Toddler Book
About Saying No (Ages 2-4).

By
Suzanne T. Christian

TWO**RAVENS**
B O O K S

**Two Little Ravens**
CHILDREN'S NON-FICTION BOOKS

Paperback Edition: 9781964202235
Hardcover Edition: 9781964202242
Digital Edition: 9781964202259

Published in the United States by Two Ravens Books LLC,
254 Chapman Rd, Ste 209, Newark DE 19702

'Expand the mind, free the imagination, one title at a time.'
**www.tworavensbooks.com**

# Welcome to
# "I Am Strong. I Say No!"

This book is a joyful collection of simple, powerful affirmations crafted for young children. As you turn each page, your little ones will discover how to stand up for themselves, speak confidently, and set healthy boundaries.

Every page features bright illustrations and everyday scenarios that encourage independence and self-awareness. By reading these affirmations regularly, your toddler can gradually strengthen their sense of security–because repetition is an excellent way to learn.

Get ready for a confidence-building journey where saying "no" becomes a positive, empowering skill for your toddler!

*Suzanne T. Christian*

"No",
helps me stay safe.

If I do not want a hug,
I say, **"No, thank you!"**

When I feel scared,
I tell a grown-up.

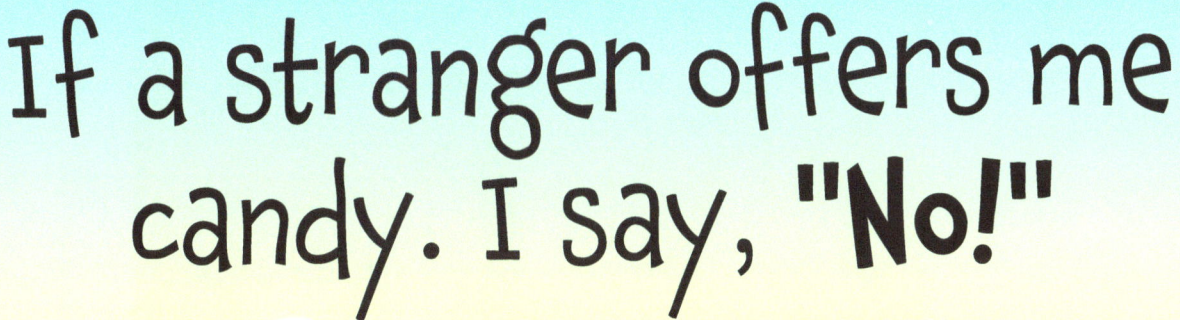

If a stranger offers me candy. I say, **"No!"**

If a friend tickles me too much, I say

HA "Stop!"

HA

HA

No is a tiny word
with big
superpowers!

If I do not like a game, I say, "No, I don't want to play."

Peas on my pizza?
No, thank you!

I am brave. I say no!

My voice is big when I say,

**"NO!"**

When I say no,
I stay safe!

I can use my hands
to show a stop sign,
then say no!

If someone doesn't stop when I say 'No,' I tell a grown-up

My feelings matter.
I say no!

My **"no"** helps me make good choices.

If someone is too rough, I say, **"No, stop!"**

No is the magic word that keeps me safe!

If a stranger offers me something, I say, "No!"

When I am tired, I say,
"No, I need rest."

# Do you like broccoli ice cream? - "No!"

I say "no" when something does not feel right.

# I Am Strong.
# I Say NO!
# The End!

# My Amazing Toddler Behavioral Series

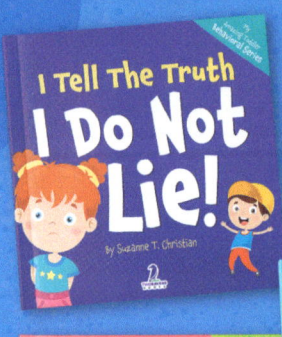
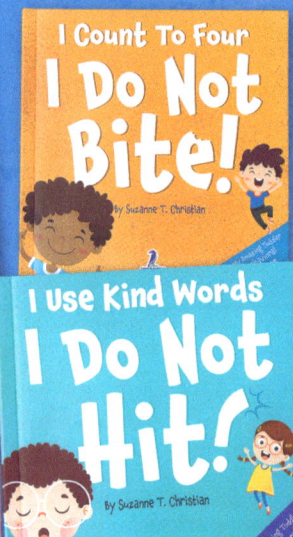
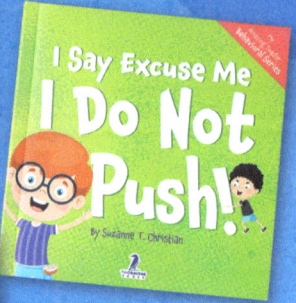
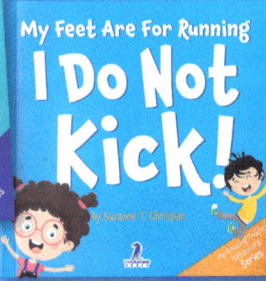

Check Out
Suzanne T. Christian's beloved series
'My Amazing Toddler Behavioral Series'.
Young readers are sure to enjoy!

## Two Little Ravens
CHILDREN'S NON-FICTION BOOKS

# Dear Amazing Reader,

Thank you for diving into **I Am Strong. I Say No!** with me. If this book touched your heart or made a difference for a young reader, I'd be grateful if you could share your thoughts in a review. Your feedback inspires my future work and helps others discover the magic within these pages.

I'd love to hear from you directly if you have suggestions or ideas for improving the book. Please feel free to reach out to me at **suzanne.christian@tworavensbooks.com.** Your voice counts, and I cherish it deeply.

With heartfelt gratitude,

www.ingramcontent.com/pod-product-compliance
Lightning Source LLC
Chambersburg PA
CBHW041437120626
46547CB00002B/252